MY AMAZING NOTERAMA

Sketch yourself here

 ADVENTUROUS

Add some words to describe yourself

GEEKY  Coolio

An Activity Journal for all ages

Helping children and adults to create Memory Snapshots of their holidays or trips

What is a Memory Snapshot?

It's capturing a moment in your time like a screen shot.
Create fun words and pictures to make your
real or imaginery memories com alive!

Think About ...

Where are you? What can you see and hear?
What are you doing? What are you feeling?

A memory keeper that brings to life a sense of place,
geography, the elements, magical mindfulness and more ...

© Helen Ann Young 2014
Hellie's World™ is a registered trademark

First published in 2014 by Young Editions, The Old Coach House TR3 6PA, UK

ISBN 978-1-908353-06-1

Illustration by Tim Blair Young and Joe Armstrong, Graphic Design by Joe Armstrong
Research Assistance Nicki John and Emily Coates

The right of Helen Ann Young to be identified as the author of this work has been asserted
in accordance with sections 77 and 78 of the Copyright Designs and Patents Act 1988.

A CIP catalogue record for this book is available from the British Library. All rights reserved.
No part of this publication may be reproduced in a retrieval system or transmitted in any form
or by any means, electronic, mechanical, photocopying, recording or otherwise without
the prior permission of the publisher or copyright owner.

Hi Everyone, it's holiday time ... yay!

We are Hellie, Sumera and Benji and delighted that you have our Amazing Noterama.

We think it's a great idea for you make your own Memory Snapshots of the exciting (or boring) things that you see, hear and do on your adventures.

Imagine how much fun it will be to read this again in 10 years time. Remember the adventures you've been on ... or imagined

Sumera used hers for a day trip to the zoo. Benji used his for his family trip to Spain and Hellie is hoping to use hers on her next magical carpet ride.

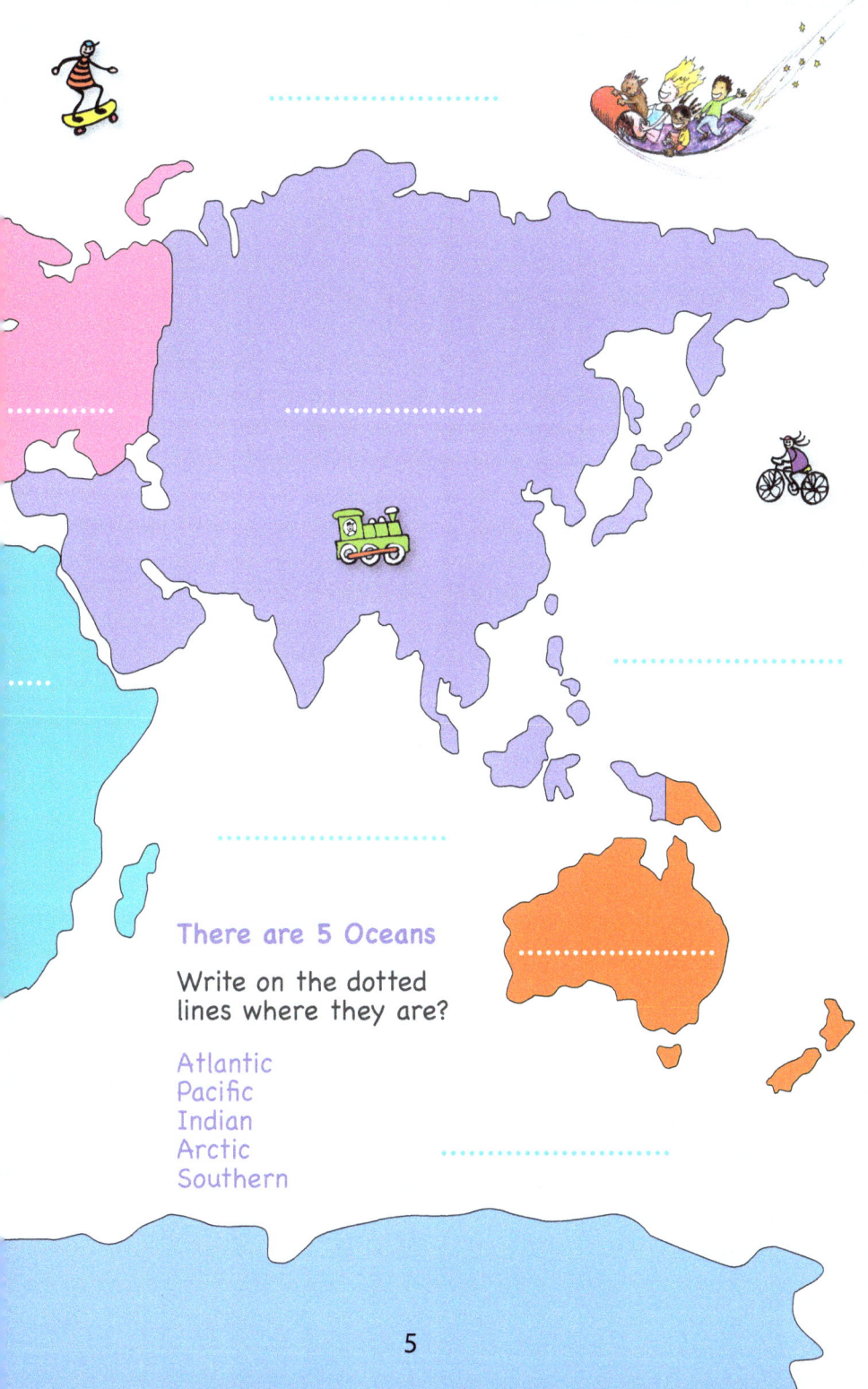

There are 5 Oceans

Write on the dotted lines where they are?

Atlantic
Pacific
Indian
Arctic
Southern

About Your Country

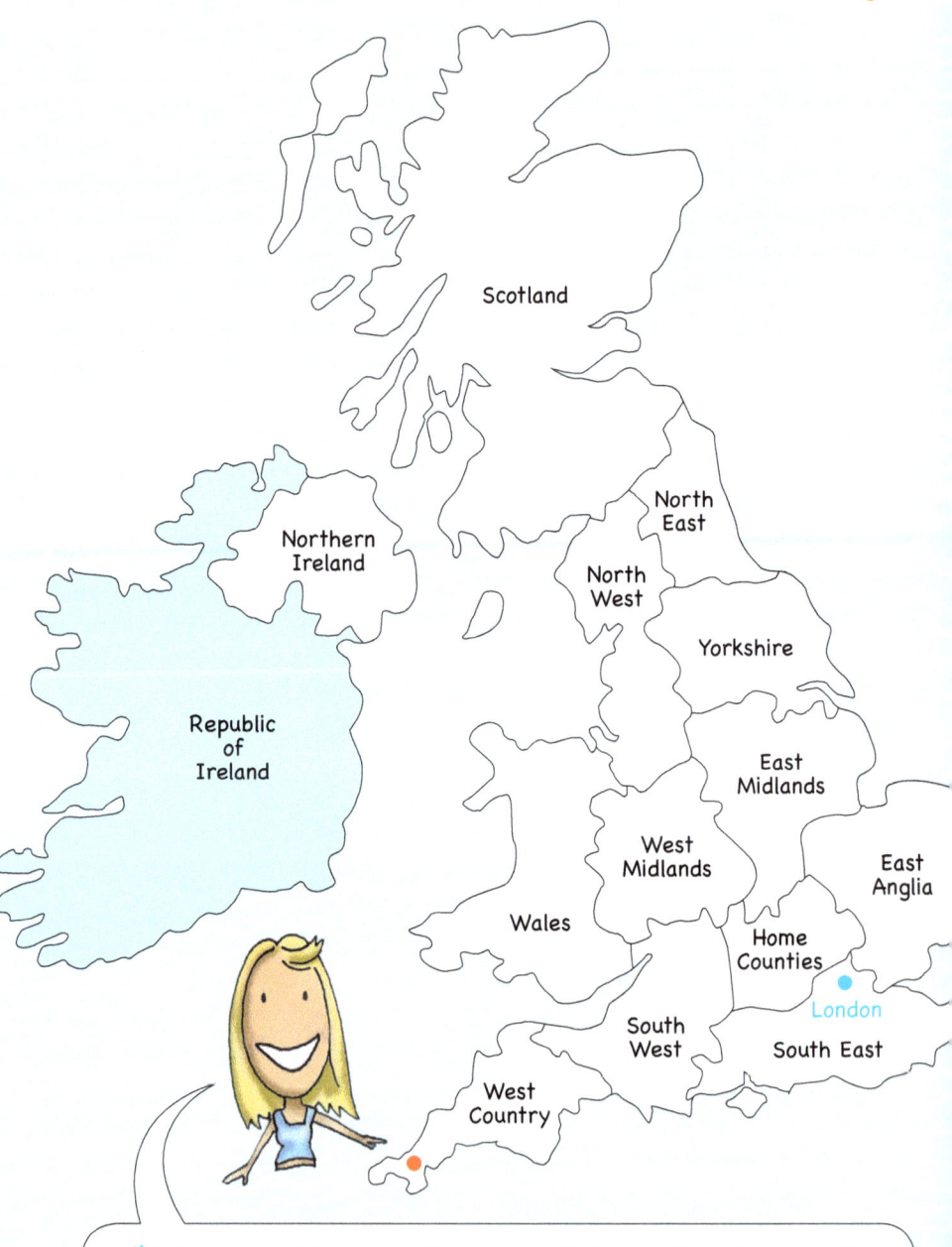

"I live right down here in Falmouth, Cornwall, which is part of the West Country of the UK"

If you live in another country draw or print an outline of your county, region or state, and stick it over the top of the map opposite.
You can even create your own imaginary country!

What is the name of your country? Colour in any regions and put a dot to show where you live.

Where is your nearest town?
Put a dot on the map and write in its name.
Hellie's nearest town is Falmouth

What is your nearest city? Add that too.

What is the name of your nearest river?
Add this as well.
Hellie's nearest river is the River Fal

Add in any important cities that you know and other towns, or rivers that you'd like.

Before you set off
on your real or imaginery trip

Where are you going and how long for?

What kind of place will you be staying in?

Who are you going with?

Have you been there before?
If so when?

How are you getting there?

Have you got some money to spend and do you know what you want to buy?

What kind of clothes, books, games are you packing to take with you?

How are you feeling before you go and why?
Draw your own expressions on page 55

Happy   Grrrr!   Worried   Sad   Giggly   Tired

Now you have arrived!
in your real or imaginery place

What's your room like?

What's the view like from your window?

How comfortable is the bed?

What's the toilet like?

Are there any markets with stalls or shopping centres nearby?

What kind of food are local people eating and have you tried some? How does it taste?
spicy, greasy, sweet, yummy, disgusting!

What language are people speaking? If you are in your own country - what accent do you hear?

What kind of people are you meeting and what are they wearing?

What's the weather like where you are?

What kind of clothes are you wearing?

How are you feeling now you've arrived and why?
Draw your own expressions on page 55

Happy

Grrrr!

Worried

Sad

Giggly

Tired

Bring your trip to life

Tune into your **5 SENSES** and give a **snapshot** of what's around you. Which of your **senses** are you using? What kind of things are you noticing?

Below are some of Hellie's examples

What can you See?
I saw the orange sunrise this morning

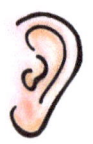
What can you Hear?
Honking car horns and screeching tyres

What can you Touch or Feel?
Slimey seaweed on the beach

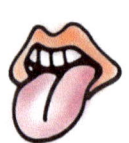
What can you Taste?
Yummy pasta and tomato sauce!

What can you Smell?
Jaffa did a nasty niff

Senses Snapshots

Hellie's Senses Snapshot

- 👁 I can see a hairy dog running into the sea
- 👂 I can hear barking and waves crashing
- ✋ I can feel the sand touching my toes
- 👅 I can taste the sea salt in the air
- 👃 I can smell chips from the cafe

Where could Hellie be?

My Senses Snapshot

Fill in your own senses snapshot

👁 ....

👂 ....

✋ ....

👅 ....

👃 ....

Where are you?

....

Colour your SENSES

Note down all the colours and shades you can see inside or outside

Note down all the smells and tastes that you've experienced today

Note down any sounds you can hear right now

Note down all the textures you can touch around you, in the room, garden or car

Bring your words alive

Here are some fun descriptive words you might like

Action	Noise	Mood	Texture
Run	Slippery	Calm	Hairy
Jump	Splodging	Relaxed	Silky Smooth
Stomp	Crunch	Chilled	Super Soft
Swim	Splat	Happy	Rough
Climb	Sneazing	Content	**Colour**
Leap	Sizzle	Dreamy	Bright Red
Twist	Giggle	Sleepy	Grim Grey
Kick	Chuckle	Grumpy	Mellow Yellow
Play	Growl	Soft	Faded Blue
Walk	Whine	Peaceful	**Taste**
Shake	Ruffff!!	Excited	Tangy
Dance	Slippery	Full on	Chilli Hot
Throw	Ahoy	Tired	Ice Cool
Catch	_ _ _ _ _	Amazed	Sickly Sweet
Wiggle	_ _ _ _ _	Made up	**Shape**
Spin	_ _ _ _ _	Cheery	Mega Big
Hop	_ _ _ _ _	_ _ _ _ _	Rock Hard
Shove	_ _ _ _ _	_ _ _ _ _	Oh So Wide!
_ _ _ _ _		_ _ _ _ _	Deep Down

Suggested Magic Words!!

Now make up your own words

Action

Noise

Mood

Texture

Taste

Shape or Colour

Word Search

```
v w p a n i z x z s o g c n
u t h u n d e r i n g l k s
s s g k l f f u b m a i s l
p m m q a i o m r r l s x r
a a c l g e l b x e k t a i
v u r n e t n l l g n e p w
b s y k g l f e i g o n o s
l n b l l r t b a i w n p f
z n q o e e q s s n v a o i
i e l k c a r c i s r v z a
l j n d g c h r y h h s o o
h w f h g i t m i v w t z c
h o c k s s g v a v s b c h
o r t l e i n g d r i p s c
l v u d x v w a l p a z q b
y v x x x u n s p e o p v l y
```

Find the word sounds hidden in the grid above

blabber	glisten	sparkle
chortle	hiss	swirl
crackle	jingle	swish
drip	pop	thundering
flowing	rumble	whisltle
galloping	snap	whoosh
giggle	snigger	zap

Word Search

```
c c h s o o z d a d s t h a
t h l r o h o h o h b w f h
g i u b i u x j s p t a a h
c n n g h u c n z d o d j h
r w a k g s c z k c z o a a
e k w l l a b e l z e h f h
a e a y c e c u s k e x t a
k h h e r b r h m i l i u a
y s w i s h y g u l t j u y
q e c w p o x n h g d q k c
y l s a l o g a s y g m o o
b k p u o t i w g k r a f l
o n w h o o f t c l v m g b
t i l h g q v k m n k s g p
j w q k r r h u v o t d r v
z t v s l f d d j a i y h m i
```

Find more word sounds hidden in the grid above

ahh ha ha	crunch	tinkle
boom	hee haw	twang
buzz	ho ho ho	twinkle
chugga chugga	hoot	whoof
clang	poof	yikes
clickety click	squelch	zoosh
creak	swishy	

19

About the 4 Elements

The elements help us to know where we are, what the weather is like and how we feel. Below are their descriptions and some of Hellie's examples.

Earth - Solid, Soil, Rocks and Buildings

What are you standing on? Where are you? What's around you?

Scrambling on the rocks
Hard concrete under my feet

Air - Movement Calm or Windy

What's the air or atmosphere like?

Steamy breath in the morning
Clouds blowing across the sky

Fire - Temperature Hot or Cold

What kind of temperature is it?

Scorching sun on my face
Glowing coals on the BBQ

Water - Liquid Wet or Dry

How wet or dry is in around you?

Raindrops pitter patter on my window
Water streaming out of the tap

Elements Snapshots

Nellie's Elements Snapshot

 I'm standing on the grass looking at flowers next to the oak tree

 The wind is blowing in my hair, it's exciting

 The sun is behind a cloud, I'm really cold

 Oh no, it's starting to rain

Where could Nellie be?

My Elements Snapshot

Add in your own

 ....

 ....

 ....

....

Where are you?

....

Elements

 How many **Earthy** things can you see?
Soil, rocks, buildings, trees ... muddy, clay, sandy

 What kind of **Air** are you noticing?
Calm, still, wild, windy ... dark clouds

What is the temperature like?
Sun, hot, cold ... fiery, icey, bbq sizzling

 How wet is it?
Drinking, rain, tap water ... sea, river, ocean

Elements, Senses and

Look at the samples and fill in your own

Benji's Snapshot

I'm in Benidorm, by the pool of our hotel. It's crowded and boiling hot! I jumped into the pool and it was freezing. We had a weird omelette for our breakfast.

SCORCHIO   **Jam Packed**   **HAHAHA!!**

Where could Benji be?

Sumera's Snapshot

I'm on the concrete looking at black and white penguins waddle about, squawking and honking for food. The metal handrail is cold. I can smell stinky, fishy water, yuk!!

SPLASH   **Pong**   **Honkk!!!**

Where could Sumera be?

Magic Words together

Grandad's Snapshot

I'm on a secret space mission. There are strange shaped rocks all around. It's very quiet - at the moment. I can see stars glittering above me and the Earth looks magical. These space gloves feel SO clumsy.

AWESOME

Watch out for Hellie's next magic carpet space adventure

My Snapshot

Where are YOU?

Snap some Mini Moments

and add some colour

Sandy
Wet   SQUIDGY!

Happy   Wet
Dog
Splashing
Yap Yap

Bring Alive a Moment

Wherever you are, stop for a minute and write down as many words as you can to describe this moment. What can you see, hear, feel ...

Red buses

Noisy Crowds

Trains whizzing

Buskers singing the same song again!!

Giant brick buildings

Big Ben chiming – Doinggg

Shops galore

Tired and Excited

People keeping eyes down

Add a sketch or photo if you like

Snap more Moments...

A Mega Moment

Some Favourite Moments

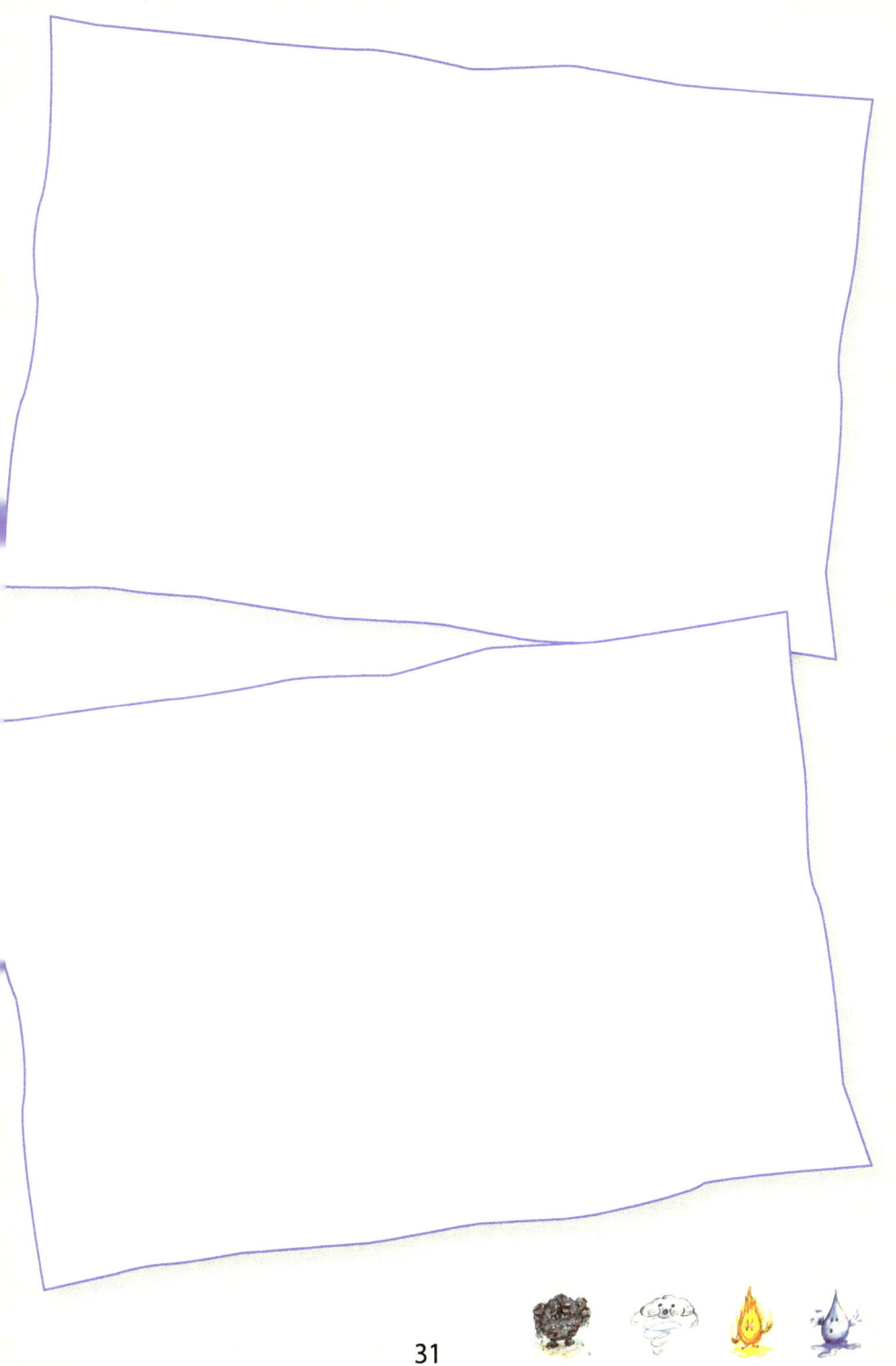

My Photos or Sketches

me feeding the giraffe

our house

Add your own sketches or photos

Have a doodle...

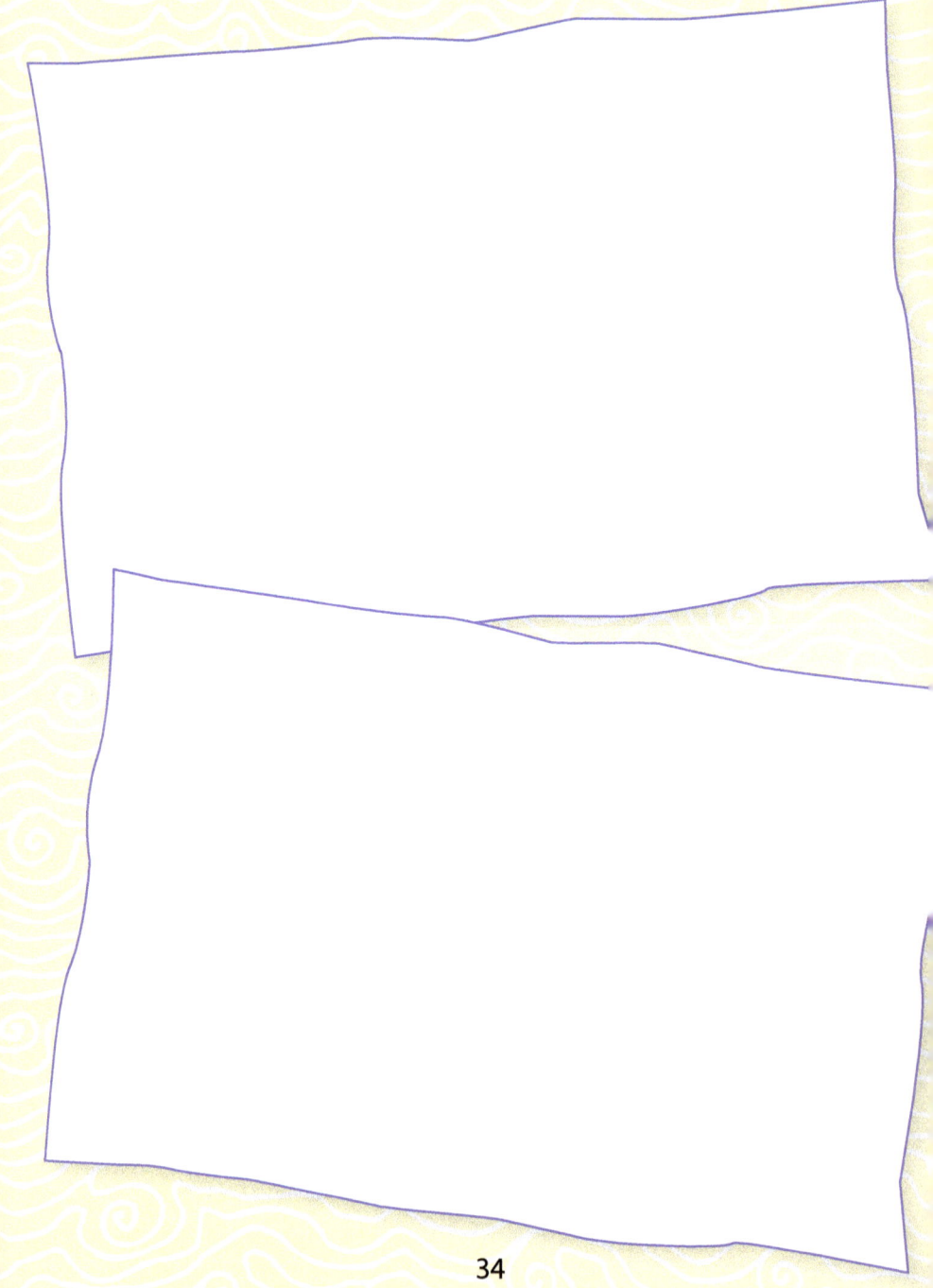

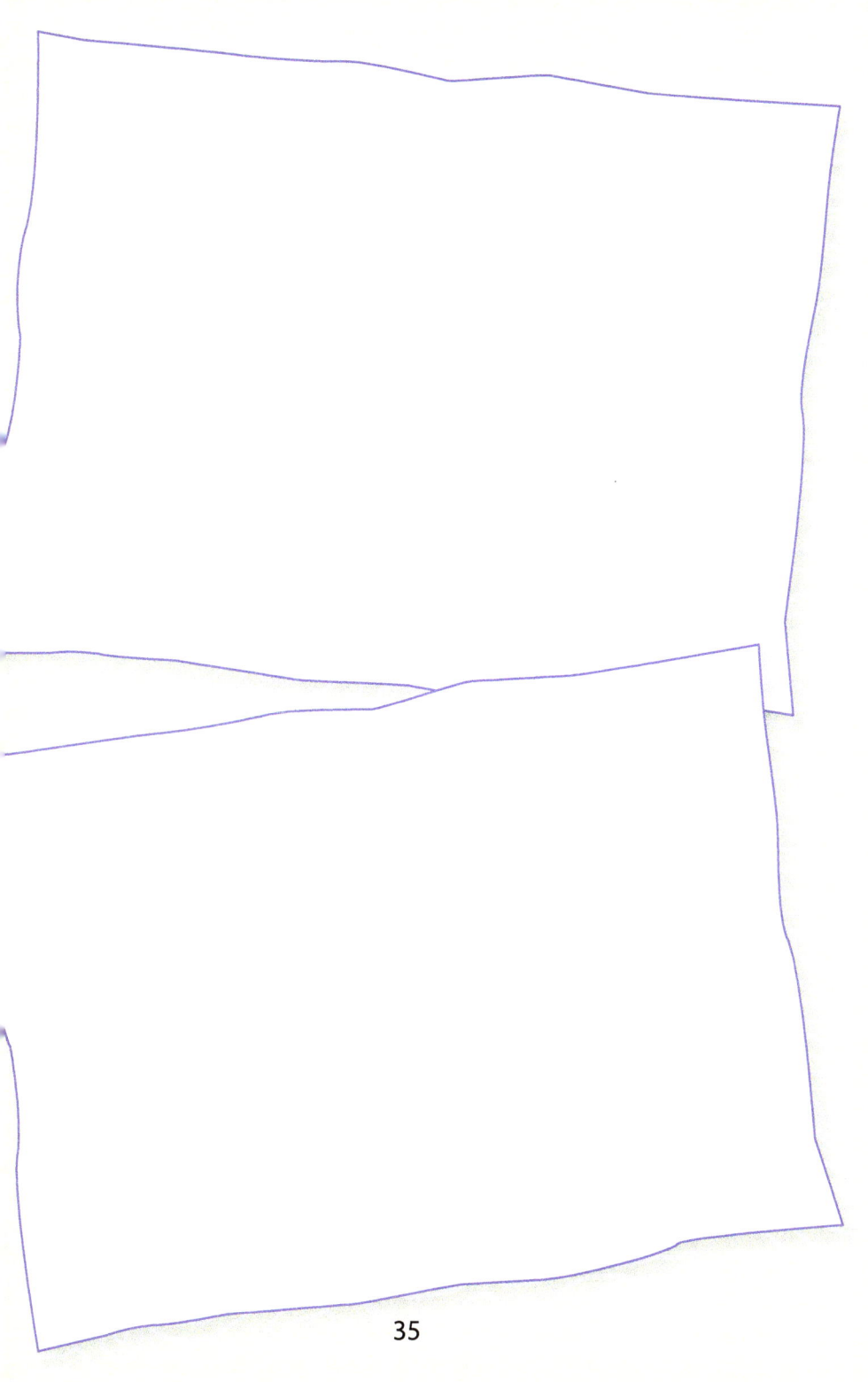

More Doodle Moments

Add your own sketches, photos and words

More diary pages

Add more of your own sketches, photos and words

Even more...

Even more of your own sketches, photos and words

Draw or write about the view from your window

What's made you laugh so far?

Draw or write about the places you're visiting

Draw or write about what you're eating and drinking

Draw or write about what you're up to

What different langauges or accents can hear around you?
Jot down some words or phrases
such as 'hola' which is Spanish for hello, or 'hello my ansome' - Cornish

Draw or write about what ever you like

MoodMaker

Create your very own Moody Faces. Add hair, beards and hats if you like.

Mapastory

Take 2 or 3 of you Snapshots and make up your own adventure story

One day...

Travel Code Puzzle

Can you work out these secret words using the Travel Codes below?

A = 1   B = 2   C = 3   D = 4   E = 5   F = 6
G = 7   H = 8   I = 9   J = 10   K = 11   L = 12
M = 13   N = 14   O = 15   P = 16   Q = 17   R = 18
S = 19   T = 20   U = 21   V = 22   W = 23   X = 24
Y = 25   Z = 26

4, 5, 16, 1, 18, 20   _ _ _ _ _ _

10, 15, 21, 18, 14, 5, 25   _ _ _ _ _ _ _

4, 5, 19, 20, 9, 14, 1, 20, 9, 15, 14   _ _ _ _ _ _ _ _ _ _ _

• •

A = 18   B = 2   C = 21   D = 9   E = 24   F = 4
G = 10   H = 20   I = 23   J = 13   K = 16   L = 12
M = 11   N = 22   O = 25   P = 17   Q = 19   R = 7
S = 26   T = 6   U = 15   V = 3   W = 8   X = 1
Y = 5   Z = 14

24, 1, 17, 12, 25, 7, 24   _ _ _ _ _ _ _

9, 23, 26, 21, 25, 3, 24, 7   _ _ _ _ _ _ _ _

18, 9, 3, 24, 22, 6, 15, 7, 24   _ _ _ _ _ _ _ _ _

Travel Code Puzzle

Now make your own Secret Travel Code below, we've given you a few words to get you started.

A =	B =	C =	D =	E =	F =
G =	H =	I =	J =	K =	L =
M =	N =	O =	P =	Q =	R =
S =	T =	U =	V =	W =	X =
Y =	Z =				

_ _ _ _ _ _ _ _ _   Cream Tea

_ _ _ _ _ _ _ _ _ _ _ _ _   Cornish Pasty

_ _ _ _ _ _ _ _   Lemonade

- -

A =	B =	C =	D =	E =	F =
G =	H =	I =	J =	K =	L =
M =	N =	O =	P =	Q =	R =
S =	T =	U =	V =	W =	X =
Y =	Z =				

New Things I've seen or done

I climbed to the top of Mt Snowdon in Wales
I swam in the sea and saw a jellyfish - ugHHH!!

Things I wish I'd seen or done

I wish I'd had a ride on a jet ski
I wish I'd seen a dolphin

My worst things

Going home, the long boring journey, & motorway food.

Write down your worst things

My favourite things

Going to the beach, eating ice cream, dinosaurs at the mueseum.

Write down your favourite things

We hope we've inspired and helped you to have fun bringing your world alive with words and pictures.

Hellie would love to hear from you.
Please share your Snap a Memories with us via Facebook, Instagram or Pinterest at ...

helliesworld.com

www.ingramcontent.com/pod-product-compliance
Lightning Source LLC
Chambersburg PA
CBHW041928040426
42444CB00018B/3462